Not As It Seems

Not As It Seems

Poems by

Pat St. Pierre

© 2021 Pat St. Pierre. All rights reserved.
This material may not be reproduced in any form, published,
reprinted, recorded, performed, broadcast,
rewritten or redistributed without
the explicit permission of Pat St. Pierre.
All such actions are strictly prohibited by law.

Cover design by Shay Culligan

Cover photograph taken in Washington, New Hampshire
by Pat St. Pierre

ISBN: 978-1-954353-73-2

Kelsay Books
502 South 1040 East, A-119
American Fork, Utah, 84003

To my three grandsons, Marc, Dylan, and Ryan
and in memory of my son Billy

Acknowledgments

Academy of the Heart and Mind: "Memories of You"

Black Poppy Review: "The Shadows"

Indiana Voice Review: "The Rainbow"

Jellyfish Whispers, Academy of the Heart and Mind: "A Turkey Hangout"

Loneliness of the Heart: "Eve Poetry"

Outlaw Poetry: "One Tiny Bottle"

Plants and Poetry Journal: "Weather Transition"

Poppy Road Review: "Family in the Red House"

Seasons of Love: "Kitchen Sink Magazine"

The Yellow Butterfly: "Intruder"

Underground Poets of Maine: "Planting Flowers"

Westward Quarterly, Highland Park Poetry: "Magical Creatures"

Contents

The Family in the Red House	11
Icy Day	12
The Shadows	13
A Turkey Hangout	14
Untold	15
The Wise One	16
Weekenders	17
Memories of You	18
Loneliness of the Heart	19
Awareness	20
Love Is Color-Blind	21
Winter Arrival	22
Not As It Seems	23
The Rainbow	24
Saying Goodbye Is Never Easy	25
Weather Transition	26
Old Photos	27
Alphabet Soup	28
The Intruder	29
Magical Creatures	30
Planting Flowers	31
One Tiny Bottle	32
The Seasons of Love	33

The Family in the Red House

While walking through woods
near a rambling river
I came upon a paint peeled red house,
barn like in appearance,
broken window panes,
tall grasses covering old cement steps—
unattended for years.
Who inhabited this red house
and where are they now?
I entered cautiously through the front door,
looked around the open space.
Dishes with cobwebs adorned a
wooden kitchen table.
Shriveled food occupied the old refrigerator.
The scene appeared as though
a family simply disappeared.
Bedroom quilts covered most beds,
one bed remained unmade.
As I walked around
floorboards creaked like soft screams.
I slipped on a small throw rug;
moving the rug with my feet,
I discovered a trap door located in the floor.
Slowly, I lifted the rusty hinge.
There in the hollow space
were skeleton bodies.
The family stayed behind in the paint peeled red house.

Icy Day

Branches from trees
sparkle like crystals.
In the sunlight
they're glossy.
Below freezing temperatures
create a wonderland of sorts.
Grass crunches under foot
and the sun is brilliant
as it glazes trees.
This winter scene happens
only occasionally.
Within a few days
branches will be bare again.

The Shadows

On this property was once a young house
occupied by a youthful woman and her family.
After many years, floor boards squeaked
and the woman's joints cracked.
It had been said, before the family
moved here, a death occurred in this dwelling.
No one was sure what had happened.
The woman, now elderly, lived here alone;
shadows seemed to move around walls at night.
At first the woman thought cataracts were her problem.
But after weeks, figures appeared in the room.
The aged woman began to question her mind and speculate
whether she was losing a part of reality.
Soft voices were heard.
They appeared to be crying. The woman's heart
pounded as she listened carefully to the sounds. A distinct
voice was heard weeping—a child's voice.
The old woman wrapped her arms around the shadow of
the child. The crying ceased. From that night
forward no figures were seen;
no voices were ever heard again.

A Turkey Hangout

Large black wings flap
as an enormous bird flies to the ground
and begins to forage on damp grass.
Other birds slowly arrive walking
across the street into a suburban yard.
Suddenly, the huge bird flaps his wings.
They open up like a colorful shawl
around his neck and body.
As he turns in place, I realize that it's a turkey
who has come to visit.
This grand bird is strutting and fanning
around the backyard—puffing for all to see.
Soon a female enters the scene.
She parades across the moist grass
with eight little chicks following her.
Perhaps these babies belong to the
majestic tom turkey as the family
gathers together for an outing.

Untold

How can I tell you,
and make you understand.
The things I should have said
can no longer be told.
How many times I tried;
I could not find the words
to thank you for your kindness,
your patience and your love.
Perhaps somehow you knew
without my mentioning the words,
or maybe you realize
as I weep and hold your hand.

The Wise One

He is wise
and sits on his regal throne
watching all subjects
sitting erect, still as a cat
going after its prey.
Is he sleeping or thinking?
He has wisdom showing on his face.
Hail, oh, great wise owl.

Weekenders

Summer residents illuminate the lake
emitting a warning to nature.
In their home away from home,
weekenders are like fireflies that
dance in the darkness.
The tranquil lake glows with
water traffic as voices
of passing boaters amplify
the lake's surface.
Fireflies glow
in the evening and
nature reigns once again.

Memories of You

Memories of you
haunt me while sleeping.
I ask myself why
they disturb me so.
I wake from memory like
dreams and fear
makes me tremble.
I want to remember
the good times
but all that enters my mind
is a fearful
memory of you.
The happy times existed
but your rage erased
all the good and created only fear.

Loneliness of the Heart

Like stripping bark off a tree
you reveal to him your most innermost thoughts.
Your soul becomes naked.
He yearns to protect you
from heartache and loneliness.
To wrap his arms
around you in comfort.
Instead,
his casual speech is noncommittal.
Faint sounds can be heard
in the distance like a foghorn
forewarning mariners of impending danger.
The magnetically charged air
causes you to uncover the pain.

Awareness

Seasons depart,
goodbyes are uttered,
farewell to katydids,
goldenrod, and bluebirds,
autumn foliage,
frost covered ground,
children leave,
lovers part,
loved ones die.

Nature's rebirth
makes the finale bearable
when relationships have ended.
Awaiting a get together
is all that's possible.

Love Is Color-Blind

An old man screams, "Don't take my wife"
as his wife's daughter from a first marriage
pulls the man's dark-skinned wife out of the room
to take her to a nursing home,
causing the old man to close his eyes,
think of his love for his wife,
and then expire with a broken heart.

Winter Arrival

In the pre-dusk evening
tree branches bend
in half almost
touching the ground
as the heavy snow
sticks to pine needles. Visibility
is poor and trees
everywhere look out of
focus and fuzzy.
Car lights on a parallel street slowly
travel down the road
looking like detached light beams.
It's in this dream-state
that a snowstorm exists.

Not As It Seems

What if you followed your heart
through rugged terrain
and over steep cliffs feeling sure that your heart
would lead you to an everlasting devotedness
only to find out that the mountainous
paths led nowhere.

How could your heart be wrong
when you were so certain
that your heart knew
where it would lead you.

The Rainbow

Rain pelts across the lake
creating shimmering circles
as a rainbow of green, yellow and red arcs across the sky.
Rain drops like berries spatter into the water.

As you close your eyes,
continuous breezes flow over your body
lifting and carrying you to unknown places—
transporting you to undiscovered islands.
You sense the heat of the sun and
you are in a safe and carefree place
when suddenly rain descends the size of nuggets
transmitting you up to the heavens.

Saying Goodbye Is Never Easy

Saying goodbye is never easy.
Goodbye to the people we love
is especially hard.
We hold on tight to memories,
we clutch them to our heart
and they lift our spirits
like wings on a bird.
Think of goodbye as only temporary.
Our mind allows us to
travel back to those special people
who mean so much to us.
It has been said "you can't go home again"
but those memories will always take you there.

Weather Transition

There's no mistake
about the season.
The weather transition is
noticeable as
night arrives earlier.
Looking out over
the lake I see
a dress parade—
trees magnificently clothed
in oranges, reds, brilliant yellows.
Nearby squirrels scamper back and forth
over some already naked trees.
But what holds my attention
across the lake
is decorated trees with
an array of colors
patiently waiting.

Old Photos

I never saw my mother smoke,
didn't smell her lingering breath
or see her brown stained teeth,
nor did I take in the stench
of smoke circling her head
and yellowish stain on her fingers.
But she kept her secret from me.
Our house was off limits to her activity
so I guess she found a different place
to engage in her pastime.
I told people who would ask,
"No my mother never smoked."
After she passed away I was looking
through old photos
and discovered her secret.
I could almost taste
the photo's smoke in my throat.
I choked from the suffocation and heaviness.

Alphabet Soup

We're making alphabet soup you and I.
Those tiny pasta alphabet letters
float in the broth
jumping up and down when boiled
like we do when we first see each other.
Noodles are bland and not spry
but you and I mesh together in exciting ways.
When the flavorful broth is poured into dishes
one can almost see happiness on the tiny pasta faces.
Is it the soup that both of us wanted
or the finished product?

The Intruder

The indifferent halls
encounter
no floral fragrance.
They bristle with death
which sticks to my uniform
and settles on my shoulder
as I walk down the corridor
on crepe-soled shoes.

Magical Creatures

Snow, snow, snow,
it's everywhere.
Wind gusts like a sand storm
trees bend and stretch
corpse like.
Moaning wind deposits more snow
on branches
turning bony trees
into magical creatures

Planting Flowers

I select my flowers carefully.
I'm not comfortable driving to the planting ground
but feel that it's not a matter of choice for me.
This is a special day for planting flowers—
Memorial Day with its small flags
waving in the breeze.
Upon arriving, I take my tools and
array of flowers and walk over to
lonely waiting gravestones.
Unkempt grounds need to be raked,
leaves and twigs have to be picked up.
I start by digging holes then choosing delicate flowers.
Most of my family is buried here
I try not to look at the names on the gravestones.
One that is the hardest to gaze at is my son's.
A wave of emotion like rolling thunder bursts forth from me.
I hug the gravestone, hurry off to the car,
as tears stream down my face.

One Tiny Bottle

How could he have known
what one small bottle
would lead to.
Pain was widespread
as it sometimes is
after surgery.
All he needed was
something to help
dull his senses.
As days moved forward
the feeling he had was delightful.
One small bottle
led to another.
In time a bottle
was necessary every day.
His appearance turned gaunt
and one day he didn't
recognize who he was.
All he could utter was
"one tiny bottle."

The Seasons of Love

It was in the autumn that we fell in love
the trees were an impressive array of colors.
As their leaves touched each other it was
almost as though the heavens opened their arms
to capture splendor for all time.
When the season turned cold and frigid
we became more distant and chilly toward each other.
We continued on afraid to end and destroy our feelings.
But when the sun started to warm the air
and spring flowers burst forth from the ground,
we had new feelings for others.
Pulsating and pushing through our hearts.
our new loves were exciting and unfamiliar.
They continued on until the intense summer heat
suffocated and smothered us.

About the Author

Pat St. Pierre is a freelance writer and amateur photographer who has been writing poetry since her high school days. Her first poem was published during college and from then on she was captivated by the written word. She has had adult and children's poetry, fiction, and nonfiction published in a variety of online and including various magazines. Some publications are in *Flutter Poetry Journal, Lutheran Parenting, Boston Literary Review, The Ekphrastic Review, Leaves of Ink, The Metaworker,* and *Poppy Road Review.* Pat's specialty is trying to capture small vignettes of life and turn them into poems. Many times photos will accompany the poems. Her topics vary from simple ordinary events to traveling down dark journeys.

This is her fourth poetry chapbook. She has had three chapbooks published by various publishers. Her first, *Reality of Life,* was published by Foothills Publishing, her second, *Theater of Life,* was published by Finishing Line Press, and her third, *Full Circle,* was published by Kelsay Books. All are available on Amazon.com.